Original title:
The Ant Philosophy

Copyright © 2024 Swan Charm
All rights reserved.

Editor: Jessica Elisabeth Luik
Author: Linda Leevike
ISBN HARDBACK: 978-9916-86-369-5
ISBN PAPERBACK: 978-9916-86-370-1

Anticipations in Ant Land

In a world beneath our feet,
Tiny cities gasp in time,
Marching lines in tuned repeat,
Rhythmic lives in silent rhyme.

Grains of sand are castles tall,
For the queens in chambers deep,
Servants answer to their call,
Dreams awoken from their sleep.

Ants with burdens, mighty loads,
Toil on through sun and rain,
Building bridges, winding roads,
Journey's end without refrain.

Through the tunnels, winding trails,
Messages in whispers pass,
Invisible, their hidden tales,
Written in the blades of grass.

Future whispers, softly speak,
Hopes in hearts they hold so grand,
In the night when stars do peek,
Anticipations in Ant Land.

Harmony in the Hustle

In the rush of the days, we find our tune,
A symphony of tasks, from dawn to noon.
Moments of calm in the swirling stream,
Life's vibrant whirl, part of the dream.

Chaos dances, as order plays,
In the harmony of our busy ways.
Every note, both high and low,
In the hustle, our spirits grow.

Silent whispers in the crowd's throng,
Each step forward, a part of the song.
Balancing acts, on tightrope thin,
In the chaos, we find peace within.

Little Legends

Tiny heroes in the garden green,
In their world, unseen but keen.
Ants and beetles, tales untold,
In courage, brave and bold.

Battles fought on leaves and earth,
Epic journeys, giving birth.
To legends small, to us unseen,
In their courage, what do we glean?

They build empires grand and wide,
In determination, side by side.
Little hearts with massive might,
In day and in quiet night.

Ants at Work

Underneath the summer sun,
A million legs, on their run.
Tiny workers, none too small,
Together, they build and haul.

In a line, they march in file,
Each one for a greater pile.
Grains of sand and leaves they bring,
A colony, their lively king.

Paths they mark with trails unseen,
Silent strength in their routine.
Harmony in every act,
Ants at work, unity intact.

Small Beings

In corners dark and shadows deep,
Where silence falls and secrets creep.
Tiny whispers, soft as breeze,
Dance with grace among the trees.

Beyond the gaze of giant eyes,
In miniature worlds of venturing wise.
Lives unfold with careful tread,
Legacies in silence spread.

Great Deeds

In the realm of whispered lore,
Where humble hearts in silence roar.
Acts of valor, strength of will,
Echo through the valleys still.

From earnest toil and steady hand,
Rise heroes grand across the land.
Mighty tales in quiet form,
Turn the tide and break the storm.

Silent Sentinels

Guardians of the night so still,
Watch the world from silent hill.
Vigilant in twilight's glow,
Secrets only they may know.

Stalwart, constant, never swayed,
In their shadows truth is laid.
Protectors of the peace they stand,
Silent oaths in every hand.

Carriers of Hope

Through the dark and stormy seas,
Guided by a whisper's breeze.
Dreams are woven, futures spun,
By the light of rising sun.

In their hearts, a bright refrain,
Promises to end the pain.
Hope's torch passed from hand to hand,
Binding together sea and land.

Busy Beneath the Surface

Underneath the lowly tread,
Lives of purpose gently spread.
Hidden hands that shape the earth,
Breath of life with whispered mirth.

Beneath the gaze so unobserved,
Tireless rhythms, undeterred.
Worlds unseen where tales unfold,
In the depths where courage's told.

Resilience in Miniature

A single seed in fertile ground,
With dreams of reaching past the sky,
Roots push down, though unseen bound,
Grows in strength, though none ask why.

Wind and storm, they test each leaf,
Raindrops fall, a sweet reprieve,
In each challenge, find relief,
In hardship, faith it will achieve.

Time will mark the seasons' change,
Growth in silence, all alone,
Through the hum of life's vast range,
Strength in subtleties is shown.

Unknown forces shape its way,
Sunlit moments, shadows cast,
Yet in darkness finds the day,
Present strength from trials past.

Small Yet Mighty

A pebble tossed in quiet stream,
Ripples out with gentle grace,
Seems so small, yet what a dream,
To alter world in peaceful pace.

Butterfly in summer's breeze,
Flutters lightly, yet so free,
Influences things unseen,
In its path, sure destiny.

Ants that march with purpose pure,
Little bodies, great in will,
Build up homes with structure sure,
Strength in numbers, can't stand still.

Small in stature, grand in might,
Counts each step with silent power,
In their realm, bring forth the light,
Mark each day, and each hour.

Purpose in a Grain

Among the sands, a grain of gold,
Lies hidden, waiting to be found,
Holds its worth in tales untold,
Glories whispered without sound.

Waves above may crash and roar,
Quiet grains withstand the strife,
Tiny testament to more,
They reflect a quiet life.

Minute dust, or cosmic star,
Both contribute to the dance,
Grains of wisdom near and far,
Small insights that life enhance.

Though unseen in grander sweep,
Each grain's purpose, vital thread,
On this journey, both wide and deep,
Each finds meaning in what's said.

Tales of the Unseen Struggle

In the soil, beneath our view,
Roots are tangled, paths entwined,
Silent battles fought anew,
Strength emerges, fiercely mined.

Beneath the bark of ancient tree,
Lies a story, rings of time,
Each small struggle, silently,
Writes a tale, both harsh and prime.

Every drop of rain must fall,
Echoes in the ground below,
In the dark, these tales recall,
Unseen struggles, growth bestow.

Quiet battles often fought,
Lead to triumphs deeply earned,
In their silence, wisdom's sought,
Hidden strength, through life discerned.

Heroics on Six Legs

In fields where shadows weave,
Ants move in tireless dance,
A kingdom they conceive,
In nature's grand expanse.

Brave soldiers on patrol,
Their paths through grass entwine,
With unity, their goal,
To build, defend, define.

Beneath the towering trees,
Their cities rise and fall,
An empire born to seize,
From summer's gentle call.

No task is deemed too small,
In their ceaseless parade,
Tiny heroes stand tall,
In sun and forest glade.

Each grain they lift and bear,
A testament to strength,
In fields where life is fair,
Their journey knows no length.

Vanguard of the Small

Purpose in every step,
A mission clear and true,
Through morning's dawn they prep,
For tasks that they pursue.

With whispers in the breeze,
They march with silent might,
Through branches, stems, and leaves,
Their efforts out of sight.

No trumpet calls their name,
No banners wave above,
Yet each accepts the same,
A duty bound by love.

United in their cause,
A bond that never breaks,
A world that often awes,
With all the risks it takes.

In tiny hearts beats pride,
For journeys long and grand,
The vanguard, side by side,
Commends the smallest hand.

The Enduring Swarm

In thrumming dusk they fly,
The air alive with wings,
A symphony on high,
As twilight softly sings.

To nectar's call they go,
Through air both thick and thin,
Through rain or even snow,
Their quest will soon begin.

A unity so deep,
In patterns, they convene,
From hovel they all leap,
A marvel to be seen.

An odyssey they weave,
In dance and swoop they share,
Their message they believe,
In movements through the air.

Come dawn, they'll still reside,
With honey in their wake,
The swarm endures the tide,
For their own kind's sweet sake.

Minute Miracles

Beneath the lofty sky,
Where giants overlook,
Tiny miracles lie,
In every cranny, nook.

From petal to the leaf,
They journey, barely seen,
In labor and relief,
Creating vibrant sheen.

With nothing less than will,
They mold their world with care,
In beauty rich and still,
Their stories fill the air.

Though small in earthly space,
Their impact echoes wide,
In every time and place,
They once again provide.

So let us pause to see,
Their efforts great and small,
In every buzzing bee,
A miracle does call.

Resilient Realms

In the heart where shadows play,
Resilient realms begin to sway.
Through storms and trials, bold and bright,
They stand untarnished, day and night.

Battles fought on fields unseen,
With courage as their evergreen.
Embrace the wounds, yet rise again,
Unyielding spirits conquering pain.

Whispers of the past may call,
Yet they march, and never fall.
Their strength, a beacon in the dark,
A guiding light, a steadfast spark.

In valleys deep and mountains high,
Resilient realms beneath the sky.
Crafted by the hands of fate,
Beyond the wrath, they navigate.

The Discipline of Tiny Feet

In the morning's golden hue,
Tiny feet with tasks to do.
A rhythm steady, step by step,
Through life's vast and endless web.

Paths are forged by careful tread,
Follow where the heart is led.
Dreams entwined with each small stride,
As they wander far and wide.

Lessons learned in silent grace,
Time, the teacher they embrace.
Discipline in every leap,
Promises they plan to keep.

In their journey, brief yet grand,
Tiny feet imprint the land.
Leaving marks of hope and cheer,
One small step for futures near.

Epic of the Earth Movers

Beneath the stars, with strength untold,
Earth movers brave, their spirits bold.
Shaping worlds with every turn,
In their souls, deep fires burn.

Mountains bow to hands of might,
As day gives birth to endless night.
Rivers flow and forests sway,
Crafted by the movers' play.

With sweat and toil, they pave the road,
Bearing every heavy load.
Legends forged in marble and stone,
Their legacy forever known.

Echoes of their deeds remain,
In the snow, in sun and rain.
Bound by duty, free from fear,
Earth movers, hold your honor dear.

Voyage of the Valiant

Across the seas where tempests roar,
Valiant hearts seek distant shore.
With sails unfurled to skies of blue,
They chase horizons, bold and true.

Waves may rise with thunder's cry,
Yet they meet with lifted eye.
Challenges in every crest,
Finding solace in the quest.

Stars as guides and winds as friends,
To the journey, there begins.
Mysteries in lands afar,
Pilgrims to the morning star.

In their chests, a fire bright,
Courage lighting up the night.
Valiant souls by fate embraced,
Voyaging to dreams unchased.

Gentle Grit

In quiet strength, her spirit grows,
Amidst the winds that fiercely blow.
Beneath the storm, her calm appears,
A beacon in the vale of fears.

With patient steps, she treads the thorn,
Through nights of shadows, feeling worn.
Yet in her heart, a fire burns bright,
Guiding her through darkest night.

Soft words and firm resolve she blends,
A lioness in love descends.
The world may test, but still she'll stand,
With gentle grit, her soul expands.

Her journey carved through time's command,
A testament to strength, unplanned.
Through every trial, she will persist,
In gentle grit, her dreams exist.

Fleeting Footsteps of Fortitude

In dawn's soft light, they start anew,
With courage in each morning dew.
Their paths diverge, yet all align,
A chorus of the brave divine.

They climb the hills of doubt and fear,
With every step, resolve is clear.
The fleeting moments of despair,
Are met with fortitude's repair.

In fleeting footsteps, strength is found,
Through every loss, a solid ground.
They march with hope, through storm's embrace,
Their spirits shine, they set the pace.

With hearts of gold and minds of steel,
They forge ahead, through woe and weal.
Resilient souls on paths untamed,
In fortitude, they are proclaimed.

Whispers Among the Sand

The desert whispers tales of old,
In grains of sand, its stories told.
Each breeze that stirs the arid land,
Unveils a secret, faintly planned.

Beneath the sun's relentless blaze,
In shadows cast by golden rays.
Echoes of journeys past remain,
Imprinted on the shifting plain.

The dunes like waves of time unfold,
A canvas brushed in hues of gold.
With every step, a tale expands,
In whispers soft among the sands.

The desert's voice, a constant low,
Of lives that wandered long ago.
Their fleeting steps through vast command,
Are murmured whispers in the sand.

Unyielding Underdogs

In shadows where the faint reside,
The underdogs with silent pride.
Though battered by the storms outside,
Within, a fire they cannot hide.

Their spirits forged in depths of night,
Emerging stronger by the fight.
Against the odds, they claw and climb,
Their will, a testament to time.

No crown nor title they possess,
Yet in their hearts, they nonetheless.
Their strength observed by few, and yet,
Their roots grow deep where dreams are set.

Resilient hearts with quiet storm,
Defying norms, they break the form.
The world may doubt, but still they rise,
In unyielding underdogs, hope flies.

Quiet Determination

In the silence of dawn, dreams ignite,
Whispers of courage start to take flight.
From the quiet comes a mighty roar,
Determined hearts will weather more.

Each step taken, no matter how small,
Becomes a journey, a valiant call.
Through valleys low and mountains high,
Steadfast spirits rise to touch the sky.

In shadows cast by doubt and fear,
Strength often builds year by year.
With every challenge faced and beat,
A quieter roar grows deep inside.

When night descends, stars softly gleam,
They hold the secrets of every dream.
For in the hushed moments, pure and true,
Quiet determination sees us through.

Grain by Grain

Grain by grain, time moves so slow,
Each moment seeds, begins to grow.
A gentle push from earth to sky,
Patience blooms where efforts lie.

The restless heart can learn to wait,
In every dawn, a new clean slate.
For greatness thrives in slow embrace,
Life's masterpieces take their place.

Through torrents, trials, and raging storms,
Each grain still holds its perfect form.
A steady beat within the chest,
Guides each effort to be its best.

With every day, a canvas fresh,
From smallest parts, a mighty mesh.
Grain by grain, the plot unfolds,
In patience, strength, and beauty molds.

Unity in Order

In unity, there's strength untold,
A tapestry of hearts grown bold.
Threads of gold and silver weave,
Harmony within, we all achieve.

Pieces fitting, one by one,
Together basking in the sun.
Order forms a seamless song,
In unity, where we belong.

From differences, a pattern blooms,
In varied shades, life fills the rooms.
With every stitch, a bond is formed,
A vision of peace, perfectly warmed.

Through order comes a mighty force,
Guided by a shared discourse.
In unity, a fracture mends,
A stronger whole, as one, ascends.

From Sand to Summit

From grains of sand to summit high,
Dreams ascend to reach the sky.
Every step, a story spun,
From dawn to dusk, and setting sun.

On paths uncertain, shadows cast,
Resilient hearts will always last.
In valleys low and peaks above,
Journey's end is paved with love.

Each challenge faced, each trial met,
Paves the way and sets the net.
With grit and grace, we climb the height,
Through darkness, striving for the light.

From sands below to summit's crest,
Passion guides our fervent quest.
With every leap, with every fall,
We rise again, standing tall.

Quintessence of Collaboration

Hands entwined in sacred dance,
Minds converge on vast expanse,
Hearts aligned in common quest,
Building dreams that stand the test.

Through the storms and past the veils,
Shared resolve knows no fails,
Fostering a boundless trust,
In unity our hopes combust.

Voices blend in harmonious song,
Together, we belong,
In collective spirit strong,
To a brighter dawn we'll throng.

Crafting visions, weaving dreams,
Thread by thread, a tapestry redeems,
Where unity's light forever beams,
Within a world of endless schemes.

Side by side we journey far,
Crossing oceans, reaching stars,
In collaboration's tender grace,
We find our place in time and space.

Minuscule Marvels

Tiny wonders, unseen sparks,
Hidden deep within the darks,
Whispers soft of life's parade,
In minutiae, splendor laid.

Petals small, in silent bloom,
Stars that twinkle in the gloom,
Minuscule, yet so profound,
In the little, vastness found.

Seashells cast upon the shore,
Nature's treasures, something more,
Wonders packed in smallest frames,
Echoes of creation's aims.

Raindrops kissing leaves with grace,
Each a world, a micro space,
Life in each detail unfurled,
Tiny marvels shape the world.

Glimpse the world in finer scales,
Where the grand in small prevails,
Marvel at the minuscule,
Life's abundance, intricate and full.

The Path of Patience

Step by step, the journey's slow,
In patience's grace, we come to know,
Time carves softly, shaping lands,
Through gentle, patient hands.

Seeds are sown in silent earth,
Growing roots of lasting worth,
Nurtured by the watchful gaze,
Blossoms bloom in time's embrace.

Mountains rise and rivers bend,
With patience, all the ways contend,
Through the trials, tempests fierce,
Steady hearts, time's edges pierce.

Eon's passage, ages wane,
Patience in the slow refrain,
Crafts the wonders, grand and vast,
From the whispers of the past.

On the path where patience leads,
Faithful hearts fulfill their needs,
In the waiting, wisdom thrives,
Patience lights the walk of lives.

Labors of Innocence

In the eyes of youth, the world anew,
Dreams and hopes come into view,
Innocence, a guiding star,
Shows us all how bright they are.

Clay and mud in tiny hands,
Castles rise on sunlit sands,
Labors pure, with joy infused,
In innocent hearts, never bruised.

Songs of childhood, melodious chime,
Untouched by the dust of time,
Building worlds with simple glee,
Crafting futures, wild and free.

In each task, a story forms,
Amid life's relentless storms,
Innocence seeks no reward,
Finds fulfillment in accord.

Blossoms of untainted hope,
Innocence, life's steady rope,
Guiding us to realms unknown,
Labors pure where souls are shown.

Quiet Strength of Ants

In shadows they dwell, out of sight,
Small beings of unyielding might.
With whispers of the earth's embrace,
They labor, leaving not a trace.

A dance of discipline, they weave,
In silent unity, they achieve.
Where weakness feared to find its place,
Bold fortitude paints every space.

Their might lies not in brazen boast,
But in the quiet—coast to coast.
Synergy in soil, life's parade,
A testament, as roots cascade.

Bound by purpose, side by side,
In harmony they coincide.
Not for glory, nor for fame,
But for the whispered, needed aim.

Lessons hidden, plain to see,
In their silent industry.
Breathing life from humble force,
Guiding nature on its course.

Tiny Architects

Beneath our feet, a world unseen,
Where tiny architects convene.
With grains of earth and unseen grace,
They sculpt their shelters in this place.

Precision marked by every move,
Designs so intricate, they prove.
In tunnels deep beneath the clay,
They carve their homes from night to day.

No grand blueprints, nor mighty cranes,
Just diligent and thoughtful strains.
Creating spaces, tight and small,
Where each and every ant stands tall.

In unity, they build as one,
Underneath the scorching sun.
Their artistry, a silent creed,
A testament to every seed.

We, the giants, walk above,
Unseen, their labyrinths of love.
In harmony with nature's breath,
They stave off both decay and death.

Miracles Underfoot

Beneath our steps, a world alive,
Where miracles in silence thrive.
Unseen by eyes, yet felt by all,
Tiny miracles heed the call.

With purpose pure, they weave the land,
In orchestrations, grand and grand.
No fanfare sounds, nor trumpets blaze,
But in their work, a bright sun's rays.

Each ant a part of grand design,
In dirt and soil, gold they find.
Connected through the earth's embrace,
Creating beauty, leaving trace.

Persistence flows through every vein,
In sun's bright light, and shadow's rain.
Their miracles transform the ground,
With ceaseless effort, cycles round.

To us, a moment blinks and fades,
For them, a lifetime's worth cascades.
Small giants in a world so grand,
Touching life with every hand.

Diligence in the Dirt

With tiny feet and steadfast hearts,
The diligent perform their parts.
In soil's embrace, they find their worth,
Transforming life within the earth.

Grain by grain, they shift, they bring
Order to where chaos would sing.
Their humble work, unseen by most,
Becomes the essence, a thriving host.

In endless march, through night and day,
They carve and build without delay.
A force united, small but fierce,
Their perseverance knows no pierce.

Through roots and rocks, they navigate,
An endless, timeless, fervent fate.
With every turn, a new design,
Their life's great work, a hidden shrine.

Grand lessons from their silent quest,
Of diligence and quiet zest.
In dirt they show, what we might miss,
The strength found in each subtle kiss.

Foragers of Faith

In hushed, green corridors, they tread,
Silent moments, prayers in stride.
Through the forests' emerald bed,
In shadows, faith and fates confide.

Beneath the vault of ancient trees,
Whispers in the cooing breeze.
Bearing burdens, light as leaves,
Hope in hearts, and minds at ease.

With every step, their spirits rise,
Unseen beneath the heavens' gaze.
In faith, they search the endless skies,
For light that shatters darkest maze.

The earth is but a fleeting stage,
Where souls can find their sacred place.
Faith sustains through every age,
Anchoring hearts in boundless grace.

In journeys wrought by mystic paths,
They venture forth, a silent trove.
With faith as foragers, surpass,
Each voyage to the realms above.

Enduring Existence

Within the hearts of time's embrace,
Exists a tale of strength unchained.
Toil and trial, met with grace,
Against the storm, they have remained.

In every wrinkle, wisdom lies,
Echoes of a life well-lived.
Through weary smiles and knowing eyes,
Endurance is the gift they give.

With every dawn, they rise anew,
Unyielding to the pull of years.
In twilight's hues, they bravely view,
The world through lenses washed by tears.

They stand beneath the weight of skies,
Undaunted by the passage swift.
The song of life that never dies,
Whispers through their spirits' lift.

In the tapestry of fate, they weave,
A testament to life's grand dance.
Enduring existence, they believe,
In every breath, a second chance.

The Minuscule Marathon

On paths unseen, the race begins,
A journey grand, in footsteps small.
Through pebble streets and grassy inns,
They march with courage, standing tall.

Each tiny stride, a giant leap,
In miniature, they brave the world.
With purpose pure and will to keep,
Their banners of resolve unfurled.

In every stretch of road and bend,
Their spirit echoes, firm and bright.
With nature as their loyal friend,
They chase the day, embrace the night.

No challenge in their eyes too grand,
They conquer peaks within their reach.
United in a common stand,
A silent lesson they beseech.

For in their toils, a truth unfolds,
That greatness lives in every heart.
And through their journey, fate beholds,
The marathon of life's fine art.

Toil in Tiny Mansions

In caverns small, with walls of clay,
They build their homes, industrious souls.
With bits of straw and night's array,
    Creating life in hidden shoals.

Through whispered halls, they navigate,
    A bustling world beneath our feet.
    In every corner, they ornate,
Their tiny mansions, calm, discreet.

With tireless claws, they shape their dreams,
In shadows cool, they weave their tales.
Through passage-ways that gleam and gleam,
    Their diligence and might prevails.

No limelight ever shines their way,
Yet grandeur frames their realm obscure.
    In tiny mansions, day by day,
They labor on, composed and pure.

In quietude their lives unfold,
    A testament to patient strife.
In mellow hues, their stories told,
    Of toil in tiny mansions' life.

Collective Grit

In the depths of hearts, resolve does flicker,
With every trial, it grows much thicker.
Together we stand, unbowed, unbroken,
In unity, strength – a truth unspoken.

Each step we take, with purpose driven,
Through storms and trials, we're never riven.
In shadows cast and battles fought,
Grit and might, by courage wrought.

With hands held firm, we face the night,
In collective will, our spirits light.
No force can break this bond we own,
For in our hearts, the fiercest stone.

Together we climb, rise from the dust,
For it's in each other that we truly trust.
In every second, hope and grit align,
A testament to this strength divine.

From dawn to dusk, we forge our way,
In unison, we face the fray.
Our collective grit, a beacon bright,
Guiding us through the longest night.

Purposeful Paths

Upon the roads, where dreams align,
We walk with purpose, arms entwined.
Each step a beat, each breath a song,
Our journey fierce, our hearts strong.

Paths diverge and twist in flight,
Yet purpose keeps us in its sight.
Through valleys deep and peaks so high,
Our destination meets the sky.

With every footfall, meaning found,
In silent whispers, purpose crowned.
No detour sways us from our quest,
For in our hearts, we are blessed.

Each choice we make, a compass true,
Guiding us through morning dew.
In darkest night or brightest morn,
Our purposeful paths are reborn.

Together we stride, hearts alight,
Chasing dreams through day and night.
In unity, our fate is sealed,
On these paths, our truths revealed.

Eternal Endeavor

In the tapestry of time we weave,
Threads of gold and silver leave.
Our efforts shine in twilight's gleam,
Eternal quests in every dream.

With each sunrise, a voice does call,
To rise once more, give it our all.
In endless cycles, we pursue,
The heights of sky, the ocean's blue.

Through trials faced and battles lost,
We learn with every step, the cost.
Yet undeterred, our spirits soar,
Eternal endeavors, we implore.

In every heart, the flame does burn,
A guiding light, our souls discern.
No mountain high, no ocean wide,
Can quell the fire deep inside.

With courage bold, and visions clear,
We chase the dreams held so dear.
In every breath, our hopes endeavor,
Forever bound, our quest – eternal.

Strength in Numbers

In unity, our strength revealed,
A force of will, our fate is sealed.
Together we rise, stand arm in arm,
A collective heart, a shared charm.

In every challenge, hand in hand,
We face the storms that life has planned.
With voices strong, our anthem sings,
The power of unity it brings.

Each life a thread in this grand weave,
Together we achieve, believe.
No single soul is left behind,
In numbers, strength and hope we find.

Through every trial, no more alone,
In numbers, we've a sturdy throne.
Our spirits lift, as one we stand,
A mighty force across the land.

Together, onward, hearts as one,
Our journey, bright beneath the sun.
In unity, we find our might,
Strength in numbers, facing night.

Tales of Micro Perseverance

In the shadow of the towering trees,
A single blade of grass sways with ease.
Against storms and the harshest breeze,
It whispers courage to the seas.

Tiny insects in the night,
Navigate by the faintest light.
Through intricate paths, out of sight,
Their journeys mark a silent fight.

Droplets on an old stone wall,
Gently gather and then fall.
With time, they conquer tall,
A testament to effort small.

Gems buried in the roughest lands,
Reveal beauty by patient hands.
Through time's shifting, drifting sands,
Their brilliance steadfastly stands.

Amidst mountains and endless sky,
A flower blooms, though ground is dry.
From cracks, it reaches up so high,
A story written by and by.

Unity in Miniature

Behold the anthill's busy hum,
Each small creature plays a drum.
Unified, though so tiny some,
Together, they are never numb.

Raindrops on a thirsty earth,
Join to bring new life its birth.
In union, they prove their worth,
Adding color, joy, and mirth.

Stars that dot the endless night,
Bringing galaxies to light.
Each little twinkle, ever bright,
Merges into one grand sight.

Petals on a rose's bloom,
Gathered in a small perfume.
In their unity, dispel gloom,
Creating space in crowded room.

Pebbles by a riverbed,
Hold up paths our feet have tread.
Side by side, though small instead,
Their bond supports where we are led.

Labors of the Little

In fields where wildflowers thrive,
Bees in hives keep dreams alive.
Each small buzz, they soon contrive,
To make the sweetest honeyed drive.

A spider spins its silver web,
Intricacies flow from every thread.
Labors small, though might be sped,
Craft designs in overhead.

Caterpillar, inch by inch,
Ascends the stem without a flinch.
Through quiet work and patient clinch,
Turns to butterfly, a colorful pinch.

In grains of soil, the seedlings fight,
Gaining strength from day to night.
Labors hidden from our sight,
Yet push through earth to seek the light.

Ants, though limbless, march in line,
Toiling always, rain or shine.
For every labor, there's a sign,
Of greatness seen in forms so fine.

Might in Miniscule Form

An emerald moss on ancient rock,
Stands undaunted by time's knock.
Firm in strength, what else can mock?
Shows miniscule might in every block.

Grains of sand on ocean coast,
Support vessels, pull and boast.
Though so small, they stand engrossed,
Bearing witness to life's roast.

A tiny bird upon the wing,
Songs of hope it dares to sing.
Despite its size, it brings the spring,
Might in motion, hearts do ring.

Fireflies in the dusky air,
Tiny beacons everywhere.
Their fleeting glows, sweet and rare,
In darkest moments, light they share.

The smallest act of heartfelt care,
Ripples out to everywhere.
Through simple gestures, joy we bear,
Might in miniscule, glowing fair.

Silent Warriors of Nature

In forests dense, where shadows creep,
A silent war does nature keep,
Insects small, with wings so bright,
Guard the day and guard the night.

They dance on petals, wings of lace,
Aerial knights with deftest grace,
Unseen battles in the air,
Protecting flora everywhere.

Their whispers blend with rustling leaves,
Crafting tales that no one grieves,
Each antenna, each delicate stride,
Keeping balance on nature's side.

With colors vivid, patterns bold,
Silent stories left untold,
Yet through their flight, the song prevails,
Guardians of the wild, tales.

In every nook, in every shade,
Where sun meets earth's embrace, they've laid,
A testament to strength so pure,
Silent warriors, steadfast, sure.

Tiny Titans

Beneath the blades of grass so green,
Lie worlds unseen, mysterious, keen,
Tiny titans, strong and true,
With mighty feats that few construe.

Ants parade in perfect line,
Strength in numbers they align,
Tireless workers, day and night,
Crafting empires out of sight.

Beetles clad in armor bright,
Radiate with ancient might,
In their shells, a tale disclosed,
Of resilience well-composed.

Fluttering wings of butterflies,
Carry hope as each one flies,
Transformations signify,
Miracles seen by the inner eye.

Tiny titans, bold and grand,
Guardians of this sprawling land,
In the micro lies immense,
Nature's perfect consequence.

Insect Inspirations

Upon the wings of dragonflies,
Glimmers of the dawn arise,
Hints of magic in their flight,
Nature's canvas, pure delight.

From caterpillar to butterfly,
A metamorphosis in the sky,
Lessons in change, profound and deep,
Insect inspirations we keep.

The humble bee, with golden hue,
Teaches teamwork, pure and true,
Through fields of bloom, they buzz and weave,
A bounty placed in each reprieve.

Crickets with their nighttime song,
Serenade the dusk till dawn,
Chirps that tell of ancient lore,
Resonating evermore.

In every meadow, grove, and glen,
Life's philosophies, we ken,
Through insects' lives, so small yet vast,
The wisdom of the ages passed.

Journey of the Industrious

From dawn's first light to setting sun,
Their journey's tasks are never done,
In fields and woods they toil and thrive,
Keeping nature's pulse alive.

Bees dart flower to flower with grace,
Their work imbues each blooming space,
Through tireless days, they churn sweet gold,
A tale of diligence retold.

Ants in tunnels deep go forth,
A testament to tireless worth,
Through grit and grind, they build and store,
Foundations strong from core to core.

Butterflies in flight, so light,
Speak of journeys, short yet bright,
Each flutter, each delicate sweep,
A chronicle they sweetly keep.

The industrious teach us well,
Of perseverance, tales they tell,
Insects small, with spirits grand,
Carving legacies in the land.

Subterranean Sagas

In tunnels deep where shadows creep,
The silent whispers guard their keep.
Roots entangle, secrets speak,
Of ancient tales that slowly seep.

Gems and stones in hidden chambers,
Craft tales of forgotten labor.
Time stands still in these dark hectares,
As echoes sing of ancient flavors.

Eyes that gleam, elusive phantoms,
In caverns carved by nature's tantrum.
Lost histories and quiet anthems,
Mark the path of chthonic fathoms.

Glowworms light the dusty ledger,
In places where the brave find pleasure.
Chronicles of buried treasure,
Unseen by the world's bright measure.

Earth-born whispers, softly woken,
Bind the untold tales, unbroken.
Each silent verse, a mystic token,
Of subterranean sagas, spoken.

The Unseen Parade

Invisible throngs with silent steps,
March through days that the world forgets.
Unheard songs in twilight's depths,
Carrying life that fate begets.

In quiet lanes where shadows blend,
An unseen parade of souls descend.
The masks they wear, they will not bend,
In echoes where lost secrets mend.

No banners fly, no trumpets blare,
Yet through the air, they weave with care.
Spectral forms in twilight's lair,
Dance unseen in whispered air.

The streets are filled with muted grace,
An unseen parade in sacred space.
Their silent hearts, a steady pace,
Invisible hands that time enbrace.

A phantom march through silvered night,
Each step a tale, each glance a light.
In shadows spun, they take their flight,
The unseen parade, hidden from sight.

March Beneath the Sun

With steadfast tread and purpose grand,
We march together, hand in hand.
Beneath the sun, on golden sand,
We chart a course across the land.

Through fields of green and mountain crest,
Our hearts with passion manifest.
Guided by light and timeless quest,
In unity, we find our rest.

No shadows cast or pathways lost,
We bear the sun at any cost.
With every step, no matter crossed,
In radiant truth, we are embossed.

The world above, a canvas wide,
We march with hope and dreams untied.
Through trials faced and moments sighed,
Beneath the sun, our spirits glide.

Each stride we take, a timeless chord,
In daylight's grace, we find reward.
Marching forward, hearts outpoured,
Beneath the sun, our souls accord.

Ants' Anthem

In narrow paths, our lives entwine,
With purpose clear, a grand design.
From dawn till dusk, we form the line,
A single heart, in task divine.

Through bustling mounds and hidden tracts,
Each tiny being never slacks.
Together strong, in countless acts,
We build our world, and none retracts.

Silent toilers, we persevere,
In labyrinths both far and near.
Though small in form, our goals are clear,
With each new dawn, we engineer.

In unity, we find our might,
Through every trial, day and night.
An anthem sung in our own rite,
Of endless work that feels so right.

With every grain and tiny stone,
We build a realm that is our own.
An ants' anthem, softly known,
A legacy by toil grown.

Realm of the Tireless

In the whispering winds, they toil unseen,
Carving dreams with hands so keen.
Stardust trails to guide their way,
In the night's embrace, they silently sway.

Every heartbeat fuels the fire,
Chasing shadows, climbing higher.
In their eyes, the cosmos spreads,
Weaving magic in golden threads.

Tireless feet on endless shores,
Searching for what life restores.
Glimmers of dawn in twilight blues,
Unbroken spirit, fate to choose.

O' noble hearts that never cease,
Finding strength in aching peace.
Under moonlight, in silken veils,
They march, their resolve never pales.

Through realms of night and day they roam,
In every heart, they build a home.
Boundless dreams and endless tries,
In the realm of the tireless, hope never dies.

Intricate Lives

Threads of life intricately twined,
Through moments lost and moments mined.
With every breath, a story weaves,
In truths and dreams, each heart believes.

Eyes like mirrors, reflections bare,
In every gaze, some love they share.
In silent whispers, secrets flow,
In their depths, life's rivers grow.

Complex webs of joy and strife,
Etched in tapestries of life.
In every touch, a universe,
In every soul, an endless verse.

Paths unknown yet intertwine,
In the garden, hearts align.
Through labyrinths of fate we glide,
In intricate lives, our spirits glide.

Moments fleeting, eternities blend,
On this journey, where dreams ascend.
Embrace the dance, the waltz of time,
In intricate lives, we find our rhyme.

Wisdom of Small Things

In the petals of a flower lies,
A secret held within the skies.
Whispers soft in the gentle breeze,
Wisdom found in smallest seas.

In a child's laughter, pure and bright,
In dew-dropped mornings, soft twilight.
In these moments, life unfolds,
Simple truths the heart beholds.

In the quiet hum of a bee,
In the rustle of an ancient tree.
Joy and sorrow, grand and small,
In these fragments, we're part of all.

Listen close to the sparrow's song,
Feel the rhythm all along.
In tiny smiles and fleeting wings,
Lie the wisdom of small things.

Ephemeral yet deeply wise,
In each sunrise, in each disguise.
In these whispers, loud and clear,
True wisdom rests, forever near.

Hidden Hustle

In the shadows, they find their fight,
Crafting dreams throughout the night.
In quiet corners, unseen strides,
The hidden hustle never hides.

Behind closed doors, ambitions fly,
In whispered prayers, and silent cry.
In the hearts that never rest,
Buried fires burn their best.

Through the darkness, hands create,
Life's symphony, intricate and great.
With every beat, they onward press,
In hidden hustle, dreams confess.

Unnoticed paths they tread alone,
In every struggle, courage is shown.
In the silence, strength is found,
In every heart, a battleground.

Unsung heroes on a quest,
Unveiling hopes in tireless zest.
In shadows deep, they light a spark,
In hidden hustle, they leave a mark.

Life in Lines

Moments fleeting, whispers in time,
Echoes of laughter, a gentle chime,
Paths converging, stories entwine,
Life in lines, a dance so fine.

Seasons turning, colors blend,
Sunrise to dusk, cycles amend,
Footprints fade, yet memories extend,
Life in lines, around each bend.

Dreams take flight, hopes arise,
Through love's lens, the spirit spies,
Trials faced, strength's disguise,
Life in lines, a myriad ties.

Time's embrace, weathered hands,
Songs of the heart, shifting sands,
Ephemeral moments, endless strands,
Life in lines, it always expands.

Legacy whispers, gentle and kind,
Imprints left, on heart and mind,
Journey unfolds, seek and find,
Life in lines, beautifully aligned.

Survival Script

Through storms we tread, with hearts of steel,
Each battle fought, wounds that heal,
Courage defines, how we deal,
Survival script, our fate we seal.

In shadows deep, where fears reside,
Hope ignites, a guiding light,
Resilience stands, side by side,
Survival script, through darkest night.

Within the fray, we find our core,
Strength awakened, to explore,
Day by day, striving for more,
Survival script, life's eternal lore.

Against all odds, we rise anew,
Oceans crossed, skies of blue,
Endurance shines, in each view,
Survival script, what we pursue.

Embrace each scar, wear them proud,
Triumph whispers, forget the crowd,
In silence loud, we are avowed,
Survival script, through pain we're endowed.

Ant Tales

Tiny beings, with noble quest,
Building homes, they do their best,
Work in unison, no time for rest,
Ant tales, nature's zest.

Lines they march, their mission clear,
Burdens on backs, they persevere,
Silent whispers, always near,
Ant tales, to us endear.

Grains of sand, each one a prize,
Labors of love, beneath the skies,
Strength in numbers, no compromise,
Ant tales, where wisdom lies.

Community strong, bonds that bind,
Teamwork's art, refined and kind,
In their world, harmony's signed,
Ant tales, a rhythm aligned.

Lessons learned, from creatures small,
Persistence, patience, above all,
In every move, there stands tall,
Ant tales, life's protocol.

Tiny Architects

Under leaves, or in plain sight,
Busy builders, day and night,
Marvels made, with skill and might,
Tiny architects, a wondrous sight.

Small but grand, their structures rise,
Nature's engineers, in disguise,
Every detail, master's prize,
Tiny architects, we idealize.

Bridges built, over morning dew,
Homes to thrive, that they accrue,
Patterns formed, stories they skew,
Tiny architects, always anew.

Beneath our feet, a bustling town,
Complex paths, nature's crown,
Crafted by those, without renown,
Tiny architects, of great renown.

In their world, design is key,
Purposeful, in symmetry,
From them, art and science see,
Tiny architects, wondrous and free.

Determined Dynamos

In the heart of every storm,
Whispers rise, a call to form.
Strength in numbers, fierce and true,
Bound by dreams, we see it through.

Hands entwined with purpose clear,
Eyes ablaze with naught to fear.
Forward march, through dark and light,
Guided by our own fierce might.

Unyielding spirits, bright suns bold,
Forge ahead; our tale is told.
Mountains yield, and rivers bend,
As our will, the world will mend.

Hope and fire, a twin refrain,
Coursing through each vibrant vein.
Together, we ignite the night,
With determined souls alight.

Every step and every breath,
Conquers fate and laughs at death.
Dynamic hearts, forever glow,
Carved in time, we persevere so.

Resilience Below

Down in valleys, shadows cast,
Resilient hearts emerge at last.
Stone and marrow, roots so deep,
Guard the dreams we vow to keep.

Underground, where whispers grow,
Life persists, despite the woe.
Silent strength in darkest night,
Rising up towards the light.

Chisels carve through earth and stone,
Fortitude in every bone.
Buried seeds, they find their way,
Breaking free to greet the day.

Trials met with steadfast grace,
Courage etched on every face.
In the soil, our spirits thrive,
Feeding hope to stay alive.

Hidden forces, power untold,
Resilience in depths so bold.
Below, we find our path to soar,
With grounded might, forevermore.

Relentless Regiment

Marching forth through storm and strife,
Bound by duty, forged in life.
Shoulder to shoulder, never fall,
Warriors strong, we heed the call.

In the trenches, shadows loom,
Yet our spirits never doom.
Voices raise in battle song,
Together, righting every wrong.

Discipline in every stride,
Valor deep, our hearts abide.
Steel and sinew, minds so clear,
Banish doubt, embrace no fear.

Onward, through the fiercest fight,
Faces set with noble light.
Relentless drive, we make our stand,
Guided by a higher hand.

With relentless hearts and steely grace,
We carve our path through time and space.
No retreat, our fervor bright,
In unity, we find our might.

Ecophenomenon

Nature's dance in vibrant hues,
Whispered secrets, morning dews.
Cycles turn, the earth in bloom,
Emerging life from winter's tomb.

Forests rise in verdant green,
Rivers sparkle, serene scene.
Winds that carry ancient tales,
Through the meadows, down the trails.

Mountains witness time unfold,
Reclaiming lands with grip so bold.
In harmony, each breath a weave,
Of ecosystems we believe.

Ocean depths, a world unseen,
Mysterious and submarine.
Coral gardens, biolights,
Reveal their wonders in the night.

Ecophenomenon takes flight,
A tapestry of pure delight.
In nature's arms, we find our place,
And cherish every wild embrace.

Persistence in a Pinpoint

In the heart of the smallest grain,
Lives a world intense and bright.
Steadfast sprout through endless rain,
Pushes skyward with all its might.

From darkness seeks the morning light,
Lifting weight of earth above.
Fragile stem in nature's fight,
No greater force than tender love.

Grains of sand, a million dreams,
Patience mold to form anew.
Of small beginnings, mighty streams,
Flow from perseverance true.

Life within the minutest speck,
Holds a story strong and vast.
From gentle roots, a trunk to stretch,
A future from the humble past.

In every pinpoint, life's grand show,
A testament to time's long climb.
From minuscule, beginnings grow,
Persistent through the trials of time.

Unseen Builders

Beneath the soil, where none can see,
Busy hands shape destiny.
Worm and beetle, ant align,
Weaving webs of life divine.

Roots extend in silent quest,
For sustenance of life's behest.
Small engineers transform the land,
Through tiny acts and subtle hand.

In darkness found, foundations laid,
Sweat and toil in their cascade.
The unseen wheel that turns the earth,
Each small creature giving birth.

Quiet labor, whispers of night,
Building worlds with silent might.
Through the ages, every breath,
Celebrates the life in death.

Microcosms bridge the gap,
Of life and death, and back again.
In unseen hands, where futures map,
The builders work in ardent strain.

Small Wonders

Tiny blooms in meadow sway,
Quiet beauty in array.
Petals soft in morning's dew,
Hold a universe in view.

Minute moments of the day,
Capture hearts in small display.
Bees that hum and birds that sing,
Marvels in the smallest thing.

Eyes that see the grander scheme,
Often miss this gentle seam.
But within each minor spark,
Lies a journey to embark.

Grains of sand on windswept shore,
Hold the essence of folklore.
In the details, wonders found,
Beauty in smallness profound.

Each slight gesture, every thread,
Weaves the fabric where dreams tread.
In the tiny, grandly see,
All the wonders life can be.

Grand Schemes

From towering heights the cities rise,
Dreams etched in glittered skies.
Steel and stone, man's grand design,
Cast in schemas large, divine.

Bridges span the roaring tides,
Roads that twist through mountainsides.
Every line a bold intent,
Charting courses, dreams invent.

In corporation halls and spires,
Plans unfold, ambitions fire.
Each keystone placed, each line aligned,
Crafting futures humankind.

Yet in the vastness, heart does find,
Purpose pure and intentions kind.
For grand schemes hold a soul within,
Breathing life through thick and thin.

From human minds such worlds emerge,
In grandeur's wake, our dreams converge.
With every step, with every stride,
Grand schemes turn the shifting tide.

Silent Symphony of Effort

In the quiet of the night,
Labors weave an unseen flight.
Hearts and minds, a silent song,
Building futures all night long.

Hands that work, though shadows gray,
Crafting dreams til break of day.
Each small effort, each firm hold,
Woven in the morning's gold.

Voices hushed, yet loud the beat,
Of wills that yearn, of hearts that meet.
In the silence, rhymes entwine,
A symphony of human sign.

Through the toiling, whispers sung,
Of hopes reborn, of tasks begun.
Silent symphony in grace,
Etches triumphs in its pace.

Though no grand applause may rise,
In quiet lanes, efforts disguise.
In each endeavor, life's full chord,
Silent symphony, our reward.

The Undeterred

Through storms and trials they are led,
With courage firm and faith ahead.
Their spirits high, their path unswayed,
In shadows deep they are unafraid.

No burden too great, no distance wide,
For hearts resolved, in trust they bide.
With every step, a testament,
To souls unbroken, resilient.

Over peaks of doubt they rise,
Steeled resolve in hopeful eyes.
Each sunrise marks a dawn anew,
Where dreams are countless, victories true.

In valleys low, in heights so high,
Their will to strive will never die.
Each challenge faced, each battle won,
The spirit of the undeterred goes on.

Through night and day, through sun and rain,
Their strength in struggle, countless gain.
With undeterred, unyielding grace,
They forge ahead, to find their place.

Underfoot Universe

Beneath our feet, a world concealed,
Where secrets hidden, are revealed.
A symphony of life below,
A dance in pathways, faintly glow.

In smallest realms, grand stories spun,
Connections made with threads unsprung.
From roots entwined to soil deep,
An underfoot universe, secrets keep.

Microscopic wonders weave,
Patterns of time, barely perceived.
In the darkened earth and shaded veils,
An ancient chronicle, never fails.

In realms unseen, yet felt so near,
The whispers of the past appear.
Each step we take, a bridge between,
The known above, the unseen scene.

Nature's lore beneath our toes,
An endless tale that softly grows.
In this profound, unseen expanse,
Lies the essence of life's dance.

Patient Procession

Along the path of time they tread,
With steps deliberate, forward spread.
Through ticking hours and days expand,
A march of moments, patiently planned.

In silence moves the great parade,
With calm persistence, hopes cascade.
No moment rushed, no second lost,
The future builds, at patience's cost.

With measured beat and steady heart,
They journey forth, no need to start.
A river's flow, a constant stream,
In patient procession, they dream.

The seasons shift, the world transforms,
Yet they persist, through trials warms.
No haste disturbs the patient's quest,
In steady cadence, they find rest.

Through years and miles, untold and wide,
They walk in faith, with time their guide.
In patience lies their strength's embrace,
A journey timeless, a gentle pace.

Grit in Grains

In fields of toil, where patience reigns,
There lies the story, grit in grains.
Each tiny seed, with hope replete,
A testament to labored feat.

From barren ground to harvest's boon,
The earth responds to farmer's tune.
With sweat and care, and hands so worn,
In simple acts, true grit is born.

Through seasons harsh and weathered trials,
They labor on with earnest smiles.
In every furrow, dream expands,
Of future's bounty, nurtured lands.

From dawn till dusk, through heat and rain,
The soul endures through ache and strain.
In every seed, a promise set,
A tale of resilience, not to forget.

Amidst the rows of sturdy grain,
They find the strength to rise again.
In fields of gold, their courage sown,
A legacy of grit, earth-grown.

Micro Marvels

In corners small where shadows creep,
Live tales of triumph, silent deep.
Tiny worlds, in detailed grace,
Micro marvels, leave no trace.

Ants that soldier in a line,
Fairy wings in moonlight shine.
Secrets wrapped in petals tight,
Beauty thrives beyond our sight.

Mossy carpets, soft and green,
Micro forests rarely seen.
Whispered winds through blades of grass,
Magic moments swiftly pass.

Jewels in dew on dawn's first light,
Beads of wonder, pure and bright.
Perfect spheres on spider's silk,
Tiny crafts, with timeless ilk.

Delicate, yet firm they stand,
Micro marvels, nature's grand.
Worlds within, a world so vast,
Present, perfect, from the past.

Grains of Grit

A single grain upon the shore,
Tells of storms and days of yore.
Grit and sand, a mighty force,
Carving cliffs through patient course.

Wind and wave in constant dance,
Smooth the edges, given chance.
Mountains bow to time's firm hand,
Yielding to the grains of sand.

Minute specks in desert's breath,
Hold the keys to life and death.
Oases bloom, where grains abide,
In their midst, the fates collide.

Grit that builds and grime that shapes,
Gives the landscape its escapes.
From the dust, new life will sprout,
Grit remains, through time's devout.

In the silence of the land,
In the tiniest granules, grand.
Grains of grit, in humble might,
Shape the earth, by day and night.

Miniscule Masterpieces

Tiny strokes and gentle hues,
Crafting worlds in morning dews.
Each small detail, a story tells,
Miniscule masterpieces in quiet spells.

Flower buds in early bloom,
Scenes within a petal's room.
Brushes dipped in sun's embrace,
Capturing beauty, face to face.

On a leaf, where droplets cling,
Nature's art in perfect ring.
Patterns formed in silent grace,
Miniscule wonders in their place.

Feathers fine with colors bright,
Wings of marvel in their flight.
Minute scales on fish that gleam,
Masterpieces in the stream.

Every thread in spider's weave,
Shows the art it can conceive.
Tiny hands of nature's clasp,
Creating wonders in their grasp.

The Tiny Taskmasters

Busy bees in golden streaks,
Harvest nectar, work for weeks.
Tiny masters of their fate,
Humming hives that never wait.

Ants that march with loads so grand,
Each a worker, grain of sand.
In their world, no task too small,
Tiny taskmasters heed the call.

Spiders in their web design,
Architects on silk so fine.
Persistent builders, day and night,
Crafting traps in silent flight.

In the soil, where roots entwine,
Mighty microbes work their line.
Decomposing, feeding earth,
Tiny hands that hold life's worth.

From the hive and beneath the ground,
Tiny taskmasters are found.
Every bit, a vital part,
Of the world's industrious heart.

Lessons from the Underdog

In shadows, strength begins to grow,
Where few would ever think to know.
Resilience blooms in darkest night,
A spark ignites, ignites the fight.

The smallest voice, so often cast,
Finds harmony, dispelling past.
In every heart, a lion's roar,
Unlocked by courage, ready to soar.

The journey long, the mountains high,
Hope fuels the wings that dare to fly.
Each stumble shapes the path ahead,
The soul is learned by where it's led.

Through challenge, grace is often gleaned,
From lost illusions, dreams redeemed.
Heroes emerge in forms unknown,
Within each trial, truth is shown.

The underdog, though less proclaimed,
In quiet pride, their spirit named.
Their triumphs come from strife endured,
A testament to hearts ensured.

Micro Miracles

In tiny dewdrops, life is spun,
A universe within each one.
Threads of silver, gleaming bright,
Whisper secrets of the night.

A flower's bloom in morning's light,
A symphony of pure delight.
The smallest acts, with love infused,
Are miracles, so often used.

Beneath our gaze, unnoticed there,
The magic of the gentle air.
Each breath, a testament to grace,
The silent wonders we embrace.

A spider's web delicately spun,
In threadbare beauty, day begun.
These micro miracles, we find,
Are treasures of the heart and mind.

In rustling leaves and songs of birds,
In quiet moments, unspoken words.
The grandeur of the simplest things,
Unseen miracles, life brings.

Building through Persistence

Brick by brick, the walls arise,
Built from dreams and steadfast tries.
Every setback, a learned way,
A foundation for another day.

With sweat and toil, the vision nears,
The fabric stitched through hopes and fears.
Each dawn a chance to forge anew,
What started small will carry through.

In patience, strength is often born,
Through nights of doubt and weary morn.
The calloused hands and aching bones,
Are monuments to seeds once sown.

Persisting through the stormy gales,
Through whispers of impending fails.
The heart beats strong against the odds,
In steadfast work, the spirit nods.

And when the summit's edge is seen,
The beauty of the journey's sheen.
Built brick by brick, with love's own hand,
Through persistence, dreams will stand.

Harmony Beneath Our Feet

Mountains tall and rivers wide,
In nature's arms, we all reside.
An orchestra beneath our feet,
With every step, the earth we greet.

Roots dig deep, in search of grace,
They intertwine in quiet space.
The ground, a tapestry of life,
A soothing balm to quell our strife.

In living soil, small creatures roam,
Each finding there a simple home.
A symphony of silent beats,
A hidden world below our streets.

Through seasons' turn and sun's embrace,
The earth's rhythm, soft and base.
Each thread of green begins to weave,
A harmony we must believe.

Respect the ground on which we tread,
For it sustains us, though unsaid.
In gratitude, our hearts should meet,
With harmony beneath our feet.

Wisdom in Tiny Steps

Wisdom comes in tiny steps,
A journey short but deep,
In each small act a lesson kept,
In silence dreams do sleep.

The ant who moves with steady grace,
Knows well the path ahead,
In every grain a world embraced,
A home within each thread.

The earth beneath tells ancient tales,
Of time and toil and might,
In every stride the heart prevails,
To chase the edge of light.

Small hands that build and craft and weave,
Create a wondrous whole,
A tapestry of what we believe,
The essence of the soul.

From dawn to dusk, we tread along,
With courage, hope, and care,
In every humble note a song,
Of dreams fulfilled, laid bare.

Silent Workers' Secrets

Beneath the sun, beneath the moon,
They toil in silent ways,
Building empires, late and soon,
In endless, driving days.

Within the soil, they carve their fate,
With whispers never heard,
Invisible yet intricate,
Bound by a single word.

Their dreams are woven into earth,
Their stories left unsung,
In every labor, a rebirth,
Of gardens fresh and young.

The secrets in their quiet hearts,
Unveil in each dawn's glow,
With every journey, new fresh starts,
In cycles old, they grow.

Yet, in their silence, lessons lie,
Of resilience, strength, and might,
A testament to how they try,
To fill the world with light.

Journey of the Diligent

In shadows cast by morning sun,
A laborer's first breath,
The journey of the diligent,
Begins with faithful steps.

Each tiny footfall marks the way,
Through forests deep and wide,
With patience making night to day,
And faith as constant guide.

No burden too immense to bear,
No trial too great to face,
For in each heart a steady prayer,
A deep and earnest grace.

The diligent, they march ahead,
Through summers and through snows,
With every fiber, every thread,
A living dream that grows.

Their paths will tell of battles won,
Of hardships met with cheer,
In every dawn a victory spun,
A testament sincere.

Whispers of the Colony

In hushed retreats, and sacred breaks,
A colony does speak,
In whispers, dreams, and silent wakes,
Their bond is pure and meek.

Through caverns long, and tunnels deep,
Their stories intertwine,
In unity, their hearts do keep,
A spirit pure, divine.

The whispers of the colony,
Are tales of earthly might,
Of working hands in harmony,
From dawn to starry night.

Each voice is but a gentle breeze,
That sways the air around,
In unity, they find their ease,
Where strength and hope are found.

So listen close, and you will find,
The wisdom they impart,
For in their whispers, ever kind,
Beats a true and noble heart.

Rhythms of Order

In the tick and tock of time, we dance
To the beat of a cosmic chance
Stars align and worlds coalesce
Under the sky's vast, endless expanse.

Nature's code in fractal design,
Shapes and patterns, so divine
Life blooms in synchronized rhyme,
Each moment a measured sign.

Harmony found in cycles of day,
Night sweeps in without delay
Earth's heartbeat, softly it plays,
Order in chaos, come what may.

Leaves whisper secrets to the wind,
Oceans' tides on moonlight tend
In every end, do we begin,
A balance taught to comprehend.

Beneath the chaos, a silent trace,
Order dwells in hidden place
Yet to see, the steady phase,
Of life's unyielding, timeless grace.

Strength in Unity

A single thread is frail and thin,
But woven tight, it holds within
The strength to bear, the might to mend,
Together, strong until the end.

Beneath the sky, the forests stand,
A unified, lush green land
Roots entwine in common plan,
Together, giants of the span.

Raindrops fall, each one alone,
Yet join and carve through solid stone
Rivers form, and oceans groan,
Lending strength to earth's backbone.

When voices rise in single tone,
Mountains move, and empires grown
A chorus loud, its power shown,
United hearts no fear hath known.

So let us gather, hand in hand,
Together, we shall firmly stand
In unity, our strength expands,
One single force, across the lands.

Inch by Inch

Step by step, and inch by inch,
Mountains climb, with steady clinch
Slow and sure, the progress made,
In measured moves, the fears all fade.

Brick by brick, and stone by stone,
Build a world, forever grown
Patience guides as seeds are sown,
In time, a mighty tree is known.

Drop by drop, the rivers flow,
Cutting paths, both high and low
Persistence in each gentle blow,
A journey's end, with purpose shown.

Word by word, a story spins,
Crafted tales where hope begins
Each chapter forming from within,
Inch by inch, the spirit wins.

Thus life unfolds in smallest parts,
A tapestry of varied arts
Achieved by careful, constant hearts,
Inch by inch, where dreams impart.

Underground Empire

Beneath the soil, a world unseen,
Where roots and creatures weave between
In darkened realms, a hidden sheen,
Of life's persistent, thriving scene.

Earthworm trails, and ant hill mounds,
Chambers deep with silent sounds
A microcosmic empire found,
In shadows, where the roots are bound.

Fungi spread in vast array,
Networks through the earth's decay
Silent kings of close-knit clay,
Ruling night and guarding day.

Larvae rest, and secrets keep,
In burrows where the memories sleep
Nourishing beds that life must reap,
An empire vast and buried deep.

So heed the call of hidden might,
In underground's dim, muted light
For in the depths, away from sight,
A world persists in ceaseless flight.

Milton Keynes UK
Ingram Content Group UK Ltd.
UKHW022015160824
447080UK00005B/71

9 789916 863695